MW00892032

TAKE A LOOK HAVE A READ

Copyright © 2023 Take A Look & Have A Read
All Rights Reserved.

Open your hands and what do you see?

Fingers!

How many fingers do you have?

You have ten of them!

You can use your
fingers to do
many things!

You can use your
fingers to feel -
the wind.

You can use your fingers
to play -
the piano.

You can use your fingers
to touch -
the fluffy rabbit.

You can accomplish so many things with your fingers!

But there is something your fingers are not meant for.

They are not meant for sucking!

Finger sucking can mess up the alignment of your teeth!

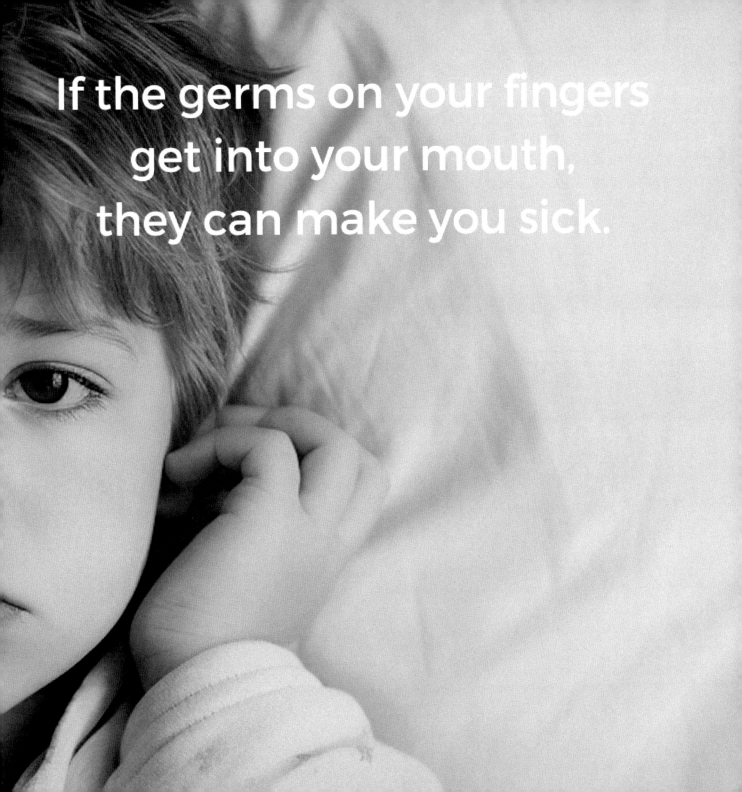

If the germs on your fingers get into your mouth, they can make you sick.

Sometimes, when you feel
bored, tired, or sad,

you may want to suck your fingers to soothe yourself.

There are other ways to make you feel better:

Hug your favourite stuffed animal!

Enjoy a popsicle!

Share your feelings
with others!

Remember, fingers are not for sucking!

Let's keep them away from your mouth, and use them to feel, play, and touch!

Made in United States
Orlando, FL
27 November 2024

54561061R10018